# Under the Mistletoe: 100 Christmas Poems

Humphrey Thorne

Published by Bright Minds Books, 2024.

While every precaution has been taken in the preparation of this book, the publisher assumes no responsibility for errors or omissions, or for damages resulting from the use of the information contained herein.

UNDER THE MISTLETOE: 100 CHRISTMAS POEMS

**First edition. November 26, 2024.**

Copyright © 2024 Humphrey Thorne.

ISBN: 979-8230692874

Written by Humphrey Thorne.

# Table of Contents


Poem 1: A Season of Love ....1

Poem 2: Beneath the Twinkling Lights....2

Poem 3: Warm Hearts in Winter's Chill ....3

Poem 4: The Glow of Friendship....4

Poem 5: Home for the Holidays....5

Poem 6: Frost-Kissed Dreams ....6

Poem 7: Silent Night, Joyful Hearts ....7

Poem 8: Magic in the Air ....8

Poem 9: Candles in the Window ....9

Poem 10: Gifts of the Heart ....10

Poem 11: Christmas Morning Glow ....11

Poem 12: The Star Above....12

Poem 13: Snowfall Serenade ....13

Poem 14: The Spirit of Giving ....14

Poem 15: Carol of the Bells ....15

Poem 16: Evergreen Dreams ....16

Poem 17: Holiday Feast ....17

Poem 18: Whispers of the Pines....18

Poem 19: Sweet Holiday Treats ....19

Poem 20: Letters to Santa ....20

Poem 21: Garland of Memories ....21

Poem 22: Fireside Tales ....22

Poem 23: Joy in Every Corner....23

Poem 24: Sleigh Bells on the Wind ....24

Poem 25: Midnight Mass....25

Poem 26: Winter's Blanket ....26

Poem 27: The Nutcracker's Tale ....27

Poem 28: The Joy of Little Things ....28

Poem 29: Christmas in the Village ....29

Poem 30: The First Snowfall ....30

Poem 31: A Candle's Flame....31

Poem 32: Christmas Eve's Embrace ........................................32

Poem 33: The Holly and the Ivy ........................................33

Poem 34: The Sound of Laughter ........................................34

Poem 35: Wishing on a Star ........................................35

Poem 36: Christmas by the Sea ........................................36

Poem 37: The Sound of Sleighs ........................................37

Poem 38: The Christmas Market ........................................38

Poem 39: The Gift of Time ........................................39

Poem 40: A Snowman's Song ........................................40

Poem 41: Under the Northern Lights ........................................41

Poem 42: The Joy of Giving ........................................42

Poem 43: The Carolers' Song ........................................43

Poem 44: Through Frosted Windows ........................................44

Poem 45: A Time for Peace ........................................45

Poem 46: A Christmas Journey ........................................46

Poem 47: Lights on the Tree ........................................47

Poem 48: The Spirit of the Season ........................................48

Poem 49: Tinsel and Tidings ........................................49

Poem 50: Echoes of the Past ........................................50

Poem 51: The Gift Beneath the Tree ........................................51

Poem 52: A Winter's Walk ........................................52

Poem 53: Christmas Magic ........................................53

Poem 54: The Bells of Christmas Eve ........................................54

Poem 55: Under the Mistletoe ........................................55

Poem 56: Christmas Candies ........................................56

Poem 57: The Stockings on the Mantel ........................................57

Poem 58: Reindeer on the Roof ........................................58

Poem 59: Wrapped in Christmas Joy ........................................59

Poem 60: The Night Before ........................................60

Poem 61: The Polar Express ........................................61

Poem 62: The Village Christmas Tree ........................................62

Poem 63: A Christmas Letter ........................................63

Poem 64: The Snow Globe's Tale ........................................64

Poem 65: The Christmas Star.................................................................65

Poem 66: The Christmas Feast ...............................................................66

Poem 67: Santa's Workshop ...................................................................67

Poem 68: The Christmas Wreath ............................................................68

Poem 69: The Quiet of Christmas Night .................................................69

Poem 70: Frost on the Windowpane .......................................................70

Poem 71: The Gift of Light .....................................................................71

Poem 72: The Chimney's Tale .................................................................72

Poem 73: Midnight Snowfall...................................................................73

Poem 74: The Joy of Togetherness ..........................................................74

Poem 75: Sleigh Ride Through the Snow.................................................75

Poem 76: The Christmas Quilt................................................................76

Poem 77: The Christmas Parade..............................................................77

Poem 78: The Sound of Christmas Morning............................................78

Poem 79: The Tree in the Square.............................................................79

Poem 80: Candy Cane Dreams ...............................................................80

Poem 81: Under Winter's Sky.................................................................81

Poem 82: The Gingerbread House...........................................................82

Poem 83: Christmas Wishes ...................................................................83

Poem 84: The Nativity Scene .................................................................84

Poem 85: The Christmas Carol ..............................................................85

Poem 86: The Christmas Lantern ...........................................................86

Poem 87: The Angel's Watch...................................................................87

Poem 88: The Ice Skaters .......................................................................88

Poem 89: The Joyful Reunion .................................................................89

Poem 90: The Christmas Candle .............................................................90

Poem 91: St. Nicholas' Visit....................................................................91

Poem 92: The Christmas Clock...............................................................92

Poem 93: The Snow Angel......................................................................93

Poem 94: The Toymaker's Gift................................................................94

Poem 95: The Holly Crown ....................................................................95

Poem 96: The Christmas Sleigh...............................................................96

Poem 97: The Fireplace Glow .................................................................97

Poem 98: The Christmas Postman ........................................................98
Poem 99: The Carol Singers ...............................................................99
Poem 100: Under the Mistletoe ....................................................... 100

**Description**

Step into the enchanting world of *Under the Mistletoe: 100 Christmas Poems.*

This heartwarming anthology of poems celebrates the spirit of Christmas through themes of love, friendship, and the magic of holiday gatherings. Each six-stanza poem captures the essence of the season, from the quiet beauty of a snowy night to the laughter shared around the fireplace.

Perfect for reading aloud with family or savoring in solitude, this collection invites readers to reflect on the timeless joy of Christmas. Let these verses inspire your holiday celebrations and remind you of the love that binds us all.

**Dedication**

This book is dedicated to those who find magic in every snowflake and warmth in every embrace. To the families who gather, the friends who reconnect, and the hearts that share laughter and love during the holiday season—you are the true spirit of Christmas. May these poems remind you of the beauty found in togetherness and the joy that shines brightest when shared.

**Preface**

The holiday season is a time of reflection, joy, and connection.

*Under the Mistletoe: A Collection of Christmas Poems* was born out of a desire to capture the magic that unfolds in these cherished moments. Each poem in this collection is a celebration of the sights, sounds, and emotions that make Christmas unique—a flickering candle, the sound of carolers, the first snowfall, or the quiet peace of Christmas Eve. Whether you seek nostalgia, comfort, or inspiration, these verses aim to stir the warmth of the season in your heart.

This book is a companion for your holiday traditions, a reminder that amidst the hustle and bustle, the true magic of Christmas lies in love and togetherness.

# Poem 1: A Season of Love

Under the mistletoe we stand,
With hearts entwined and hand in hand.
The world adorned in red and white,
A scene of joy on Christmas night.
The fire glows, a gentle hum,
The scent of pine and cinnamon.
Together here, our spirits sing,
In love's embrace, eternal spring.
Snowflakes fall in soft embrace,
They mirror stars in heaven's space.
With every kiss, a wish takes flight,
To spread this warmth through winter's night.
A wreath upon the old front door,
Reminds us what we're thankful for.
In every hug, in every cheer,
We find new love each passing year.
The season brings a gentle grace,
A tranquil joy in every place.
We gather close, both young and old,
To share our hearts as tales are told.
So let us cherish every sight,
The candle's glow, the silent night.
For Christmas lives where love does grow,
Under the gentle mistletoe.

# Poem 2: Beneath the Twinkling Lights

The tree stands tall, its branches wide,
With ornaments we place with pride.
Each light that twinkles, warm and bright,
Illuminates this holy night.
Our laughter rings, it fills the air,
A melody beyond compare.
In every smile, in every song,
We find the place where we belong.
The scent of cookies fresh and sweet,
The sound of carols on the street.
A magic lingers, calm and true,
A wondrous peace comes into view.
Beneath the starry Christmas sky,
We pause to let the year slip by.
For in this moment, hearts align,
And love transcends both space and time.
A child's gaze with pure delight,
Reflects the joy of twinkling light.
Through innocent and hopeful eyes,
The spirit of the season flies.
So gather near, let moments stay,
Hold tight to those who make your day.
For Christmas glows with love so bright,
Beneath the shining, twinkling light.

# Poem 3: Warm Hearts in Winter's Chill

The frost may bite, the winds may wail,
But warmth within will never fail.
A cozy fire, a hearty cheer,
Brings comfort as the snow draws near.
Through icy panes, the world is white,
Yet hearts indoors are filled with light.
For every laugh, and every grin,
Keeps out the cold, lets joy begin.
Scarves and mittens, bundled tight,
We venture forth through snowy night.
Yet hand in hand, we feel no cold,
Together brave, together bold.
A cup of cocoa, steaming sweet,
Warms frozen hands and chilly feet.
In every sip, in every smile,
We linger here a little while.
The chill of winter can't suppress,
The bonds of love we now express.
For hearts once warmed by holiday cheer,
Can brave the frost throughout the year.
So let the winds howl if they may,
Inside, our love will light the way.
Through winter's chill, we stand as one,
Until the morning brings the sun.

# Poem 4: The Glow of Friendship

Around the table, friends unite,
With laughter loud and faces bright.
Each story told, each joke that's shared,
Shows just how much our hearts have cared.
The bonds we've built through passing years,
Through trials faced, through joy and tears,
Are strengthened in this festive glow,
A love that only friends can know.
The clink of glasses, cheerful chime,
We toast to friendship, love, and time.
For every season, near or far,
True friends remain our guiding star.
No gift can match the warmth we feel,
When friendships true are strong and real.
Together here, we share our cheer,
And welcome in another year.
Through Christmas past and Christmas new,
Our friendships hold both firm and true.
And under twinkling lights tonight,
We bask in bonds of pure delight.
So raise a glass and sing a song,
To friendships deep, both old and strong.
For Christmas brings the brightest light,
When shared with friends, all hearts ignite.

# Poem 5: Home for the Holidays

The train arrives, the car pulls near,
Familiar sights, familiar cheer.
A wreath adorned with ribbons bright,
Greets us on this Christmas night.
The hallway echoes with delight,
As hugs are given, faces light.
No matter where we choose to roam,
Our hearts will always lead us home.
The table's set, the candles glow,
The feast awaits, a joyous show.
With every dish and every bite,
We taste the love that feels so right.
The hearthstone warms, the stockings hang,
While voices raise, a carol sang.
In every room, in every space,
We find the love of this embrace.
Though journeys take us far and wide,
We cherish moments side by side.
For home is more than wood and stone,
It's love and laughter fully grown.
So let us treasure what we see,
This holiday with family.
For home's a gift that's wrapped in care,
A Christmas love beyond compare.

# Poem 6: Frost-Kissed Dreams

The snow falls soft, a gentle veil,
Its beauty tells a winter tale.
Each flake that lands, a whispered dream,
Reflecting moonlight's silver gleam.
Through frosted glass, the world stands still,
A wonderland of pure goodwill.
Beneath the stars, our dreams take flight,
On this serene and silent night.
The world adorned in winter's white,
Holds dreams of warmth and love tonight.
For even in this frost-kissed cold,
Our hopes and wishes shine like gold.
Each step we take on snowy ground,
Brings joy in every crunching sound.
And though the air is crisp and clear,
Our hearts are filled with holiday cheer.
So as we rest in winter's glow,
Our dreams take shape in falling snow.
For Christmas night, though calm it seems,
Is filled with magic, frost-kissed dreams.

# Poem 7: Silent Night, Joyful Hearts

The night is calm, the world at peace,
All worries fade, all troubles cease.
Beneath the stars so pure, so bright,
Our hearts find joy on this soft night.
A carol hums through frosty air,
Its melody beyond compare.
The world adorned in winter's sheen,
Creates a tranquil, wondrous scene.
We gather close, no need for words,
Just quiet hums of distant birds.
In silence, love speaks loud and clear,
A bond that grows with every year.
The twinkle lights in windows gleam,
Reflecting every hopeful dream.
While nature whispers soft and low,
Of peace the season longs to show.
Through stillness, joy begins to rise,
It lights our souls and clears our eyes.
For Christmas night, so calm, so true,
Reminds us love will see us through.
So as the world is wrapped in white,
We cherish peace this silent night.
And hold this joy within our hearts,
As every Christmas day departs.

# Poem 8: Magic in the Air

There's magic swirling through the skies,
In every flake that softly flies.
A special glow, a gentle spark,
That brightens even winter's dark.
The air is filled with sweet delight,
With every breath, our hearts feel light.
It lingers in the songs we sing,
And dances in the bells that ring.
Each house adorned with festive cheer,
A beacon shining bright and clear.
The magic grows with every smile,
Transforming hearts all the while.
The children's eyes, so wide, so bright,
Reflect the magic of the night.
In every laugh, in every cheer,
The spirit of the season's near.
It's more than lights, or gifts, or snow,
It's something deep that makes us glow.
A love that reaches far and wide,
And fills the world with warmth inside.
So let the magic fill your heart,
A wondrous gift the world imparts.
For Christmas brings a joy so rare,
A season with pure magic in the air.

# Poem 9: Candles in the Window

A candle flickers in the dark,
Its gentle flame, a hopeful spark.
It lights the way for all to see,
A beacon of serenity.
Each window holds a glowing light,
That warms the chill of winter's night.
A symbol of the love we share,
And all the ways we show we care.
The shadows dance upon the wall,
Their rhythmic sway enchants us all.
And in their glow, our hearts ignite,
With peace that shines so pure, so bright.
Each candle tells a silent tale,
Of journeys past, of love unveiled.
Its steady flame, a quiet guide,
To lead us where our dreams reside.
Through snow and storm, the light remains,
A steadfast glow in windowpanes.
It calls us home, to warmth and cheer,
To Christmas joy that draws us near.
So let your candle brightly burn,
A guiding light for all who yearn.
For in its glow, the world will find,
A peace that calms both heart and mind.

# Poem 10: Gifts of the Heart

The finest gifts aren't wrapped in bows,
They're felt within, where true love grows.
They can't be bought, they can't be sold,
They shine with warmth, more pure than gold.
A gentle word, a kind embrace,
A smile that lights a weary face.
These simple acts, so small, so true,
Are gifts that give the whole year through.
No box or ribbon can contain,
The joy they bring through snow and rain.
For gifts of heart and love sincere,
Bring Christmas magic ever near.
The joy of giving, pure and sweet,
Is found in every act we meet.
From helping hands to whispered cheers,
These gifts will last beyond the years.
So as we gather, young and old,
Let's cherish gifts that can't be sold.
For love and kindness, freely shared,
Are Christmas gifts beyond compare.
Let hearts be full, let spirits soar,
And spread these gifts from door to door.
For in these treasures, we will find,
The truest joy for all mankind.

# Poem 11: Christmas Morning Glow

The morning breaks, the dawn is here,
A day of joy, a day of cheer.
The world awakes to bells that ring,
And songs of hope the angels sing.
The tree stands proud, with gifts below,
Its lights reflect a morning glow.
Excitement stirs, as voices rise,
With laughter sparkling in their eyes.
The air is filled with sweet delight,
As morning turns to golden light.
Each gift unwrapped, each moment shared,
Shows just how much our hearts have cared.
The joy of children fills the room,
A light that chases winter's gloom.
Their happiness, so pure, so true,
Renews the season's magic too.
With every hug, with every cheer,
We welcome love that's ever near.
For Christmas morning shines so bright,
With warmth and peace, a true delight.
So let this glow remain all year,
A guiding light both bright and clear.
For every morning, hearts can show,
The love we find in Christmas glow.

# Poem 12: The Star Above

A star above, so clear, so bright,
It guides us on this holy night.
Its shining rays, a path they trace,
To lead us to a sacred place.
Beneath its glow, the world is still,
A quiet peace, a gentle thrill.
It whispers softly through the skies,
A song of hope that never dies.
The shepherds watch, the wise men roam,
This star will guide their journey home.
Its brilliance cuts through darkest skies,
A beacon where true wonder lies.
In every heart, its light does gleam,
A spark of love, a cherished dream.
It calls us all, both near and far,
To follow its eternal star.
Let every home its light embrace,
Let every soul find joy and grace.
For Christmas shines in skies above,
A star of peace, a star of love.
So as we gaze in awe tonight,
Let hearts be lifted by its light.
And may its glow forever guide,
Our lives with love this Christmastide.

# Poem 13: Snowfall Serenade

The snow descends, a quiet song,
Its gentle rhythm plays all night long.
Each flake a note, a soft refrain,
A melody on windowpane.
The world is hushed, a canvas white,
A masterpiece of pure delight.
Its beauty sings in whispers low,
A serenade of falling snow.
We watch the dance, a peaceful sway,
As winter writes her grand ballet.
The air is crisp, the silence deep,
A tranquil tune that lulls to sleep.
The snowfall's song, both soft and true,
Brings peace to all, both me and you.
It wraps the earth in calm embrace,
And fills our hearts with gentle grace.
So let us listen, near and far,
To nature's quiet, snowy star.
For in this serenade, we find,
A harmony for heart and mind.
The snowfall sings, its tune so sweet,
A Christmas hymn, a pure retreat.
And in its song, we are restored,
By winter's love, forever poured.

# Poem 14: The Spirit of Giving

The spirit of giving fills the air,
A kindness shown, a love we share.
No greater gift than this we find,
The joy of giving, warm and kind.
A helping hand, a gentle deed,
A heart that meets another's need.
These acts of love, so pure, so bright,
Bring hope to all on Christmas night.
The gifts we wrap may bring delight,
But those we give from hearts ignite.
A spark of joy that spreads afar,
A light within, our guiding star.
In every smile, in every cheer,
The spirit grows, it draws us near.
For Christmas gives us all the chance,
To let our love and joy enhance.
So let us give with open heart,
And play our role, our humble part.
For in this giving, we receive,
A love so true, a faith believed.
The spirit lives beyond this day,
In every act, in every way.
Let Christmas shine where we are driven,
Through every gift of love, we've given.

# Poem 15: Carol of the Bells

The bells ring out through frosty air,
Their joyous chimes beyond compare.
Each note a call, a cheerful sound,
That spreads its joy the world around.
They echo through the town below,
A melody both soft and slow.
Then rising high, they lift the night,
And fill our hearts with pure delight.
The carol sings of peace and love,
A harmony from skies above.
It beckons all to gather near,
To share in Christmas joy and cheer.
With every ring, with every tone,
The bells remind we're not alone.
Their song connects us, far and wide,
And keeps the spirit by our side.
So let us sing with voices strong,
And let their message linger long.
For in the bells, a truth is found,
A love that knows no earthly bound.
The carol plays, its sweet refrain,
A tune of hope, a soft refrain.
And in its chime, the world can see,
A season bright with harmony.

# Poem 16: Evergreen Dreams

The evergreen stands proud and tall,
A symbol loved by one and all.
Its boughs adorned with shining light,
Reflect the joy of Christmas night.
Through every year, its needles stay,
A promise that it won't decay.
It whispers soft, a timeless song,
Of hope and love, so pure, so strong.
Beneath its branches, gifts we lay,
A token of this festive day.
Its beauty speaks of life that's true,
A constant green in winter's hue.
The star atop, it shines so bright,
A guiding beam in darkest night.
Its light reminds us to believe,
In miracles we can't perceive.
The evergreen, a steadfast friend,
Its message clear, its roots extend.
Through every storm, through every breeze,
It stands as strong as mighty seas.
So may its dreams inspire us all,
To rise each time we fear we'll fall.
For Christmas brings eternal cheer,
In evergreen dreams, year after year.

# Poem 17: Holiday Feast

The table's set, the candles glow,
A feast prepared, a joyful show.
With every dish, with every plate,
We gather round and celebrate.
The scent of spices fills the air,
A banquet made with love and care.
From savory bites to sweets divine,
Each moment shared, each laugh a sign.
We pass the bread, we raise a toast,
To friends and family, cherished most.
In every sip, in every cheer,
We taste the love that draws us near.
The clatter soft, the stories told,
Of Christmas memories, young and old.
Each bite a blessing, rich and true,
A gift of love from me to you.
So let us savor every part,
A holiday feast that warms the heart.
For in this gathering, we find,
A joy that lingers in our mind.
The meal may end, the plates be bare,
But Christmas leaves its love to share.
And every feast will bring to light,
The bonds we hold on this great night.

# Poem 18: Whispers of the Pines

The pines stand tall, their branches sway,
They whisper secrets, far away.
Through chilly winds, their voices rise,
A song that echoes through the skies.
They hum of winters long gone by,
Of starry nights and snowy sighs.
Their needles catch the soft moonlight,
And shimmer gently in the night.
Beneath their shade, the earth lies still,
A peaceful calm on every hill.
Their scent, so fresh, it fills the air,
A Christmas gift beyond compare.
The forest sings in quiet tune,
Beneath the gaze of silver moon.
Its harmony, a gentle plea,
To cherish love and family.
So let us pause and listen well,
To every tale the pines do tell.
For in their whispers, we may find,
The peace and joy for heart and mind.
Their song of love, both deep and pure,
Will in our hearts for e'er endure.
And through the pines, the world will see,
The spirit of eternity.

# Poem 19: Sweet Holiday Treats

The kitchen hums with joy and cheer,
As holiday delights appear.
With sugar dust and cinnamon,
The season's baking has begun.
The cookies bake, their scent so sweet,
A tempting, festive Christmas treat.
The gingerbread, the candy cane,
Bring smiles to all who can't refrain.
We roll the dough, we shape with care,
Our laughter fills the frosty air.
For every taste, for every bite,
A memory made on Christmas night.
The table gleams with pies and more,
A sight to make our spirits soar.
Each treat a gift of love and cheer,
A taste of joy this time of year.
So as we share these sweets divine,
We toast to love, our hearts align.
For Christmas treats, though small they seem,
Create a bond, a cherished dream.
Let's savor every crumb and bite,
And spread the joy of this delight.
For every treat is made with care,
A holiday gift beyond compare.

# Poem 20: Letters to Santa

The letters fly on winds so swift,
Each one a child's heartfelt gift.
With hopes and dreams, they're written tight,
And sent to Santa through the night.
Dear Santa, bring a toy for me,
Or something nice beneath the tree.
But more than gifts, we ask you please,
To spread your joy across the seas.
The chimney waits, the cookies set,
For Santa we will not forget.
His jolly laugh, his cheerful face,
Brings magic to each hearth and place.
Each letter holds a secret wish,
A simple toy, a favorite dish.
But hidden in each line and plea,
Is love for all, both you and me.
So as he reads, his heart will swell,
With joy no words could ever tell.
For every child, both near and far,
Shines brightly like a Christmas star.
Let's write with hope, let dreams take flight,
For Santa reads on Christmas night.
And every wish he takes to heart,
Is where true Christmas magic starts.

# Poem 21: Garland of Memories

The garland drapes the banister,
With memories of years that were.
Each ribbon tied, each bow in place,
Reflects a time we can't replace.
The sparkling beads, the strands of light,
They twinkle soft in winter's night.
And as we gaze, the past unfolds,
In stories of the love it holds.
A cherished heirloom here and there,
Reminds us of the love we share.
For every twist, for every braid,
A memory is gently laid.
The garland speaks of Christmas past,
Of moments sweet that ever last.
Through laughter bright, through gentle tears,
It carries love through all the years.
So let it shine, so bright, so clear,
A beacon for the ones we hold dear.
For Christmas garlands softly weave,
A tale of joy that we believe.
With every year, its beauty grows,
As love through every household flows.
A garland bright, of hopes and dreams,
A ribboned path through life's great streams.

# Poem 22: Fireside Tales

The fire crackles, embers glow,
As outside falls the silent snow.
We gather close, our voices blend,
In stories told that never end.
The tales of Christmas long ago,
Of carolers singing in the snow.
Of journeys made through ice and sleet,
To bring loved ones a gift so sweet.
The elders speak of simpler times,
Of snowy hills and church bell chimes.
Their voices warm, their eyes alight,
With memories of a Christmas bright.
Each story paints a vivid scene,
Of kindness shown, of moments serene.
Through every word, our hearts embrace,
The joy and love of Christmas grace.
So let us sit by fire's warm glow,
And let the tales of old bestow,
A sense of peace, a feeling true,
That Christmas past still lives in you.
For every ember softly hums,
Of joy that lasts when winter comes.
And in each tale, we find our way,
To cherish every Christmas Day.

# Poem 23: Joy in Every Corner

The house is trimmed from floor to beam,
A Christmas wonderland, it seems.
Each corner holds a festive flair,
A little joy placed here and there.
The stockings hang above the fire,
Their presence sparks a warm desire.
To share the love this season brings,
Through every act, our spirit sings.
The windows frame a frosted view,
Where candles shine and dreams renew.
Each little nook, a treasure bright,
Transforms the home on Christmas night.
The scents of pine and spice abound,
As carols play their merry sound.
Each note and scent, a warm embrace,
That fills our hearts, that fills our space.
From every room, from every sight,
The season sparkles pure and bright.
It whispers softly, sweet and clear,
That Christmas joy is ever near.
So may our homes forever be,
A place of love and harmony.
For every corner, filled with cheer,
Will keep the Christmas spirit here.

# Poem 24: Sleigh Bells on the Wind

A distant sound through frosty air,
The sleigh bells ring, beyond compare.
Their chime, a call to young and old,
A melody both bright and bold.
They jingle softly through the trees,
A rhythm carried by the breeze.
And as they sing, our hearts take flight,
Through snowy fields, in pure delight.
The sleigh glides swift, a shadow fleet,
With gifts and joy for all to meet.
Its journey spans both near and far,
Guided by a shining star.
The horses neigh, their breath like mist,
As winter weaves her frosty twist.
Yet on they go, their bells in tune,
Beneath the light of Christmas moon.
So listen close when night is still,
For sleigh bells ringing o'er the hill.
Their sound, a promise we hold tight,
Of love and peace on Christmas night.
Let hearts be light, let spirits soar,
As sleigh bells echo evermore.
For in their chime, we come to find,
The joy of Christmas intertwined.

# Poem 25: Midnight Mass

The church bells toll, the time is near,
For midnight Mass, we gather here.
Through snow and cold, our steps are light,
To honor Christ this holy night.
The candles flicker, soft and low,
A golden warmth through pews they throw.
Their light reflects on faces near,
All gathered close in Christmas cheer.
The hymns arise, a sacred song,
A melody both pure and strong.
Each voice unites in harmony,
A prayer for love and unity.
The sermon speaks of peace and grace,
Of kindness shown in every place.
A message clear, so softly told,
That warms the heart through winter's cold.
As Mass concludes, we step outside,
Beneath the stars, our spirits wide.
For Christmas brings a joy profound,
In every heart, it can be found.
So let us keep this faith in sight,
Through every day, through every night.
For Christmas lives where love is shown,
In hearts that make its grace their own.

# Poem 26: Winter's Blanket

A blanket spreads o'er field and hill,
Its touch so soft, its hush so still.
A snowy quilt, both pure and white,
Transforms the world on Christmas night.
The trees adorned in frosty lace,
Bring winter's charm to every place.
Each branch a work of art so fine,
A masterpiece of Christmastime.
The rooftops glisten in the light,
Reflecting stars that shine so bright.
While every path and garden's bloom,
Lie sleeping in their winter's room.
The world is wrapped in peaceful rest,
A season's gift, its quiet best.
And in this calm, we pause and see,
The beauty of simplicity.
So let this blanket's quiet glow,
Remind us all of love's soft flow.
For under snow, the seeds remain,
To bloom anew in spring's refrain.
Let hearts be still, let peace abound,
In every snowflake softly found.
For Christmas brings a soothing grace,
That blankets all in warm embrace.

# Poem 27: The Nutcracker's Tale

The stage is set, the lights aglow,
The Nutcracker begins its show.
A tale of wonder, dreams, and cheer,
That fills our hearts this time of year.
The music swells, the curtains rise,
A kingdom forms before our eyes.
With twirls and leaps, the dancers play,
A Christmas story on display.
The prince, so brave, with heart so true,
Through magic lands, his journey flew.
With Clara by his side, they find,
A world of joy, a love entwined.
The Sugar Plum's sweet melody,
Delights the crowd in harmony.
Each note and step, a wondrous sight,
That lifts our souls on Christmas night.
As curtains fall, the crowd erupts,
With joy that swells and never stops.
For Nutcracker's tale reminds us all,
Of Christmas magic, standing tall.
So let its story linger near,
A cherished part of every year.
For in its dance, we come to see,
The timeless joy of family.

# Poem 28: The Joy of Little Things

It's in the small things Christmas lives,
In every smile, in all it gives.
A handmade card, a hug so tight,
These little things bring pure delight.
The sparkle of a child's eyes,
When seeing gifts that bring surprise.
The sound of laughter, warm and true,
A simple act that changes you.
A quiet walk through snowy streets,
A shared embrace when loved ones meet.
A mug of cocoa by the fire,
These little joys we all desire.
The beauty in a single star,
That shines its light from worlds afar.
A snowflake landing on your hand,
A fleeting touch, a moment grand.
It's not the grandeur, not the show,
But in these moments, love will grow.
For Christmas thrives in simple ways,
In little things that light our days.
So cherish each small joy you find,
For they will linger in your mind.
And let these little blessings bring,
The sweetest notes of Christmas sing.

# Poem 29: Christmas in the Village

The village square is trimmed with care,
With wreaths and ribbons everywhere.
The lamplights glow with golden hue,
As carolers sing melodies true.
The cobbled streets with snow are lined,
Each home aglow, their warmth combined.
The baker's shop, its windows bright,
Entices all on this cold night.
The children skate on frozen pond,
Their laughter lights a joyful bond.
While sleighs go gliding through the snow,
With bells that jingle as they go.
The church bell tolls, its echo clear,
A call to all who gather near.
To share in peace, to spread the light,
And celebrate this Christmas night.
The village hums with love and cheer,
A festive joy we hold so dear.
And as the stars shine high above,
The village glows with Christmas love.
So may this charm forever stay,
To warm our hearts on Christmas Day.
For Christmas in the village bright,
Brings timeless joy and sweet delight.

# Poem 30: The First Snowfall

The first snow falls in soft embrace,
It blankets earth in purest grace.
A quiet peace, a gentle cheer,
Announces that the season's here.
The children rush to see the sight,
Their laughter fills the frosty night.
With mittened hands, they shape the snow,
Creating wonders as they go.
The snowflakes twirl in playful dance,
A fleeting moment, a winter trance.
They land on rooftops, fields, and trees,
A gift delivered on the breeze.
The world transforms, a wonderland,
As winter paints with careful hand.
Each flake a brushstroke, soft and bright,
A masterpiece of sheer delight.
So as we watch the snowflakes fall,
Let's cherish this, the first of all.
For in its beauty, hearts will know,
The magic of the year's first snow.
Let winter's peace and joy remain,
A quiet song, a sweet refrain.
For Christmas starts with snow's first light,
And fills the world with calm and white.

# Poem 31: A Candle's Flame

A single candle's gentle glow,
Can light the dark and calm the woe.
Its flicker soft, its warmth so near,
Brings hope and peace this time of year.
The wax drips slow, the shadows play,
A quiet light to guide our way.
It speaks of love in silent tone,
A warmth that reaches every home.
In every room, its light will shine,
A beacon bright, a gift divine.
It calls us near, it draws us close,
To cherish all we love the most.
The candle's flame, a fragile spark,
Dispels the fear within the dark.
And as it burns, it softly sings,
Of Christmas joy and wondrous things.
So light a candle, let it glow,
And watch its peaceful warmth bestow.
For in its light, we come to see,
The beauty of tranquility.
Let every flame this Christmas Eve,
Remind us all of what we believe.
For candles burn with love's pure name,
And Christmas lives in every flame.

# Poem 32: Christmas Eve's Embrace

The night is still, the stars are bright,
The world prepares for morning light.
On Christmas Eve, we hold so near,
The ones we love, the ones we cheer.
The stockings hang by fire's warm glow,
The tree stands proud, adorned with snow.
And in the air, a quiet peace,
As every heart feels joy's release.
We gather close, with stories told,
Of Christmas magic, young and old.
The laughter soft, the whispers sweet,
Make Christmas Eve feel so complete.
The hours pass, the night grows deep,
As little ones drift off to sleep.
Their dreams of wonder take their flight,
Through Christmas skies of purest light.
And as we sit in soft repose,
Our hearts are filled with love that grows.
For Christmas Eve's a time of grace,
A tender, timeless, warm embrace.
So let us treasure moments rare,
With those we love and truly care.
For Christmas Eve will always be,
A night of love and harmony.

# Poem 33: The Holly and the Ivy

The holly bright, with berries red,
Adorns the halls and wreaths ahead.
Its leaves, so sharp, its spirit bold,
A Christmas tale of ages old.
Beside it stands the humble ivy,
Its green a symbol, strong and lively.
Together, they in beauty blend,
A message clear: love has no end.
The holly sings of courage true,
Of strength through storms and mornings new.
The ivy climbs with gentle grace,
A faithful friend in every place.
They decorate both hearth and door,
A festive welcome evermore.
Their presence brings both peace and cheer,
A symbol of the season dear.
Through winter's chill, their colors stay,
A sign that love won't fade away.
For holly and ivy hand in hand,
Bring Christmas joy to every land.
So may their story live and grow,
In every heart, through frost and snow.
For holly's red and ivy's green,
Remind us what true love can mean.

# Poem 34: The Sound of Laughter

The sound of laughter fills the air,
A melody beyond compare.
It echoes through the frosty night,
A joyful tune, a pure delight.
Around the hearth, the stories flow,
Of Christmas past, of long ago.
Each chuckle brings a memory bright,
That warms our hearts on winter's night.
The children's giggles, soft and sweet,
Are music that makes life complete.
Their playful joy, their shining eyes,
Reflect the love that never dies.
The elders laugh with knowing smiles,
Their mirth erases time and miles.
For in their hearts, the spirit stays,
A timeless gift from Christmas days.
Let laughter be our guiding light,
Through every storm, through every fight.
For in its sound, we come to see,
The bonds of love and family.
So laugh aloud, let spirits soar,
Let joy resound forevermore.
For Christmas thrives in every cheer,
And laughter keeps its spirit near.

# Poem 35: Wishing on a Star

A single star shines high and bright,
It guides us on this holy night.
Its steady beam, so strong, so true,
A light of hope for me and you.
We close our eyes and make a wish,
For love and peace, a world of bliss.
The star above will hear our plea,
And carry it across the sea.
Its light connects both near and far,
A universal Christmas star.
It tells a tale of long ago,
Of love that set the world aglow.
Through every age, its light remains,
To heal the heart, to soothe the pains.
And as we gaze with hopeful eyes,
Our dreams take flight into the skies.
So let us wish with all our might,
On this clear, calm, and sacred night.
For every star that shines above,
Reminds us of eternal love.
And as the Christmas dawn draws near,
Let starlight guide our hearts with cheer.
For in its glow, we come to see,
The beauty of eternity.

# Poem 36: Christmas by the Sea

The waves roll in, a rhythmic sound,
A Christmas peace that knows no bound.
The moonlight dances on the tide,
As stars align and worlds collide.
The salty breeze, the ocean's song,
It carries love both deep and strong.
The lighthouse glows, its beam of light,
A Christmas star for ships in flight.
The sand is cold beneath our feet,
Yet hearts are warm, the night is sweet.
We gather close, we sing aloud,
As ocean waves applaud the crowd.
The sea reflects the season's cheer,
Its depths remind us love is near.
Through crashing waves and gentle foam,
The spirit finds its way back home.
So let us cherish moments rare,
Of Christmas by the ocean's care.
For even here, where tides may rise,
The season's magic never dies.
With every wave, with every breeze,
Christmas lives in hearts with ease.
By sea or shore, we're bound as one,
Till morning light and day begun.

# Poem 37: The Sound of Sleighs

A distant sound, a jingle clear,
It signals Santa's time is near.
The sleigh glides swift through frosted skies,
Its bells a chorus that never dies.
Through snowy woods, through quiet towns,
It weaves its path, it knows no bounds.
Each chime a promise, pure and sweet,
Of joy and gifts for all to meet.
The reindeer fly with graceful might,
Their hooves a blur in endless flight.
While Santa laughs, his voice so jolly,
Bringing cheer with every folly.
The rooftops blur as sleigh bells ring,
A wondrous sound that makes hearts sing.
For on this night, the world will see,
A magic born of mystery.
So as we sleep, we hold in sight,
The sleigh that soars through Christmas night.
Its sound, a melody so true,
That binds the old and brings the new.
Let sleigh bells ring, let hearts be light,
For Christmas soars on wings of flight.
And in their sound, the world will find,
A joy that lingers in the mind.

# Poem 38: The Christmas Market

The market hums with bustling cheer,
A festive joy that draws us near.
With every stall, with every light,
The town transforms on Christmas night.
The scent of spices fills the air,
Of roasted nuts and treats to share.
The laughter rings, the children play,
As shoppers search for gifts to lay.
The artisans with skillful hands,
Create their wares for distant lands.
Each ornament, each crafted toy,
Brings Christmas magic, endless joy.
The choirs sing, their voices rise,
Their carols echo through the skies.
A simple tune, a sweet refrain,
That brings us back to love again.
The market glows with warmth and light,
A beacon in the frosty night.
And in its heart, we come to see,
The beauty of community.
So let us cherish every part,
The market's charm, its beating heart.
For Christmas lives in every stall,
A festive joy for one and all.

# Poem 39: The Gift of Time

The greatest gift is one unseen,
A treasure vast, a space serene.
It's time we spend with those we love,
A gift that's sent from realms above.
A moment shared, a laugh, a smile,
Can linger with us all the while.
Through fleeting days and winter's chill,
The gift of time can warm us still.
No ribbons wrap this gift of gold,
Its worth surpasses treasures old.
For in its span, we come to know,
A love that only time can show.
So let us give this gift with care,
A moment here, a presence there.
For every second freely shared,
Is proof of how much hearts have cared.
The holidays remind us all,
To answer every loving call.
For time is precious, pure, and true,
A gift that binds both me and you.
So hold this gift, let moments stay,
And share its light on Christmas Day.
For time with loved ones, spent in cheer,
Is what makes Christmas bright and dear.

# Poem 40: A Snowman's Song

The snowman stands with cheerful grin,
A top hat perched, a scarf tucked in.
With eyes of coal and carrot nose,
He stands as winter's magic shows.
The children laugh, their joy so loud,
As snowflakes fall in gentle shroud.
They sing and dance around their friend,
A Christmas tune that knows no end.
The snowman smiles, his silent cheer,
Reflects the love that gathers near.
For in his form, a bond is made,
A fleeting joy that won't soon fade.
The world may change, the seasons turn,
Yet winter's song will still return.
Each snowman built with love and care,
Reminds us of the joy we share.
Though spring may come and snowmen melt,
The warmth of friendship still is felt.
For every flake, each snowy part,
Leaves lasting prints upon the heart.
So sing along, let voices rise,
With snowman's song beneath the skies.
For Christmas brings a tune so sweet,
That even snowmen can't compete.

# Poem 41: Under the Northern Lights

The skies alight with colors grand,
A Christmas show by nature's hand.
The northern lights in splendor gleam,
A dancing, swirling, vivid dream.
Beneath their glow, the snowfields shine,
A scene that feels almost divine.
Their shifting hues, from green to gold,
A story of the heavens told.
The quiet hum of winter's night,
Is matched by this celestial sight.
A moment rare, a view so vast,
That ties the present to the past.
We stand in awe, our hearts aligned,
With beauty that transcends the mind.
For in these lights, we see a grace,
That fills the world in every space.
So let us treasure skies so bright,
This gift of nature's pure delight.
For under northern lights we see,
A glimpse of Christmas' majesty.
Let every hue, let every glow,
Remind us of the love we know.
And may the lights forever shine,
A Christmas gift, a sign divine.

# Poem 42: The Joy of Giving

The joy of giving fills the air,
A precious act, a love we share.
It's in the thought, the heart, the care,
A gift of kindness everywhere.
A knitted scarf, a homemade pie,
A gentle hug, a lullaby.
Each offering, though small it seems,
Carries the weight of heartfelt dreams.
The joy of giving isn't bound,
By ribbons tied or treasures found.
It lives in gestures, pure and true,
A selfless act from me to you.
For every gift, both big and small,
Can lift a spirit, warm us all.
And through these acts, we come to know,
The light of love that starts to grow.
So let this joy within us stay,
And guide us through each passing day.
For Christmas thrives when hearts are living,
In the simple, wondrous joy of giving.
Let every gift, both near and far,
Become a bright and shining star.
For in the joy of giving's glow,
A world of peace begins to grow.

# Poem 43: The Carolers' Song

A knock upon the frosted door,
Then voices sing of Christmas lore.
The carolers, with hearts so bright,
Bring warmth and joy to winter's night.
Their songs of peace, their hymns of cheer,
Remind us all that love is near.
Through every note, a story told,
Of Christmas wonders, new and old.
Their melodies drift through the air,
A gift of hope beyond compare.
And as they sing with voices true,
They spread the light to me and you.
The stars above join in their song,
A harmony both deep and strong.
And in the silence of the snow,
Their music makes the world aglow.
So may we sing, and may we find,
A song of love for all mankind.
For carolers bring a joy so sweet,
That every heart they warmly greet.
Let voices rise, let spirits soar,
And echo through each open door.
For in their song, the world can see,
The beauty of community.

# Poem 44: Through Frosted Windows

Through frosted windows, scenes unfold,
Of tales both cherished and retold.
A world adorned in icy lace,
Reflects the magic time can't erase.
We watch as children play in snow,
Their laughter pure, their faces glow.
A snowball fight, a sledding race,
Brings life to winter's quiet grace.
The candles flicker in the night,
Their golden glow a calming sight.
Through frosted glass, their light appears,
A symbol of the love we hold dear.
The world beyond, though cold it seems,
Is filled with warmth, with hope, with dreams.
Each flake that falls, each gentle breeze,
Creates a peace that softly frees.
Through frosted panes, we come to see,
A glimpse of Christmas harmony.
For in the quiet, snow-filled land,
The love of Christmas takes its stand.
So let us pause and gaze a while,
Through frosted windows, hearts will smile.
For every scene, both near and far,
Holds Christmas magic, like a star.

# Poem 45: A Time for Peace

Christmas brings a time for peace,
A calm where all our troubles cease.
The world adorned in purest white,
Reflects the hope of this clear night.
The wars may rage, the storms may blow,
But Christmas brings a gentle glow.
A moment's pause, a breath of air,
A time when love is everywhere.
The bells that ring, the hymns that rise,
Proclaim a truth that never dies.
For peace begins within the heart,
A gift that every soul imparts.
Let every hand reach out to mend,
And turn a stranger to a friend.
For in this peace, the world can see,
A path to true serenity.
So may this season's peaceful light,
Guide us beyond this holy night.
And as the years and days unfold,
Let peace remain, both strong and bold.
For Christmas gifts, both great and small,
Are crowned by peace, the best of all.
A time for love, a time for grace,
A time for peace in every place.

# Poem 46: A Christmas Journey

A journey starts on Christmas Eve,
With dreams in tow, and hearts that believe.
Through snowy paths and starlit skies,
A Christmas wonder before us lies.
We travel far, through fields and towns,
Through forests deep and snowy downs.
Each step we take, a story grows,
Of love and joy that Christmas shows.
The lanterns guide our merry way,
As songs of cheer help light our stay.
And in each home, a welcome warm,
We find a shelter from the storm.
The journey's end, a place of peace,
Where love and laughter never cease.
A family gathered, young and old,
Their bond more precious than pure gold.
Though journeys vary year by year,
The heart of Christmas stays so near.
For every path, through frost and flame,
Leads back to love that stays the same.
So let us journey, hand in hand,
Through every snow-kissed Christmas land.
For in our travels, we will find,
The joy of Christmas intertwined.

# Poem 47: Lights on the Tree

The Christmas tree stands tall and grand,
Adorned with lights by careful hand.
Each twinkle tells a story bright,
Of love and hope on this clear night.
The strands of gold, the orbs of red,
Bring life to boughs where dreams are spread.
A star atop, it gleams with pride,
A beacon through the night, our guide.
The lights reflect on faces near,
Their glow brings joy and Christmas cheer.
Through every twinkle, hearts will see,
The magic of the Christmas tree.
Around its base, the gifts are laid,
But it's the light that love conveyed.
For in its glow, we come to find,
A peace that settles every mind.
So let the tree shine ever clear,
A symbol of the love we share.
For lights that dance on branches green,
Are Christmas blessings, softly seen.
With every twinkle, every gleam,
The tree fulfills a Christmas dream.
A light that warms, a light that stays,
To guide us through the holiday's maze.

# Poem 48: The Spirit of the Season

The spirit of the season grows,
In every heart, its magic flows.
A quiet joy, a gentle grace,
Transforms each home, each sacred space.
It's in the songs that children sing,
The laughter shared, the church bells' ring.
In every smile, in every cheer,
The spirit whispers, love is near.
It brightens halls with candlelight,
And warms the coldest winter night.
It guides our steps, it lifts our voice,
And makes each moment one of choice.
To give, to share, to lend a hand,
To spread love wide across the land.
For in this season, hearts align,
With acts of kindness, pure, divine.
The spirit lingers, calm and clear,
Through every Christmas, year to year.
A gift unseen, yet deeply known,
A love that makes the world feel home.
So let this spirit fill your days,
And light your path through life's great maze.
For Christmas lives where hearts do shine,
In every soul, a spark divine.

# Poem 49: Tinsel and Tidings

The tinsel drapes with sparkling glow,
A shimmering touch on boughs below.
It catches light, reflects the cheer,
A golden thread of Christmas near.
With every strand, with every gleam,
The tree becomes a wondrous dream.
Its branches hold a magic true,
A world of joy for me and you.
The tidings come from far and wide,
Of peace and love this Christmastide.
They fill the air, they touch the heart,
A message that we all impart.
For tinsel shines but once a year,
Yet leaves behind its glowing cheer.
It reminds us all, both near and far,
Of who we are and who we are.
So may your days with tinsel gleam,
With laughter light and peaceful dream.
And may the tidings softly ring,
A Christmas hymn that makes hearts sing.
For in this season, joy will grow,
Through tinsel's shine and hearts aglow.
A festive time, a loving call,
A season bright for one and all.

# Poem 50: Echoes of the Past

The echoes of the past draw near,
As Christmas songs ring soft and clear.
Each melody, a gentle guide,
Through memories of times we've tried.
The laughter shared in years gone by,
The Christmas feasts, the snowy sky.
Each echo brings a tear, a smile,
A memory cherished all the while.
The faces of those we hold dear,
Seem closer still this time of year.
Their love remains, a constant light,
That guides us through the darkest night.
The past and present intertwine,
In every carol, every chime.
And through these echoes, soft and sweet,
Our hearts with loved ones always meet.
So as we gather, let us cheer,
For Christmas past still lingers near.
It lives in love that's built to last,
In echoes from the seasons past.
May every song, may every bell,
Remind us all of stories we'll tell.
For Christmas spans both near and far,
A timeless gift, our guiding star.

# Poem 51: The Gift Beneath the Tree

Beneath the tree, a gift is laid,
Its simple wrap with care displayed.
No ribbon bright, no shining bow,
Yet holds a love we all will know.
It's not a toy, or gold, or gem,
But something meant for all of them.
A token small, yet deep and wide,
A Christmas love none can divide.
The gift is time, a chance to share,
A moment pure, beyond compare.
To sit, to laugh, to simply be,
The greatest gift for you and me.
Its value grows with every year,
A treasure built on love and cheer.
For time together, spent in joy,
Surpasses any worldly toy.
So as we gaze upon the tree,
Let's not forget what gifts can be.
For love and time are treasures true,
A Christmas gift from me to you.
Let every present underneath,
Bring joy that makes our hearts believe.
For gifts of love, though simply wrapped,
Hold magic, pure and everlasting.

# Poem 52: A Winter's Walk

Through snowy woods, we softly tread,
The path before us lightly spread.
The world is still, the air is clear,
A winter's walk brings Christmas near.
The trees stand tall in frosty white,
Their branches glisten in the light.
Each step we take, each breath we make,
Feels like a dream, a gentle wake.
The silence speaks in quiet tone,
Of nature's peace, of love unknown.
And in this walk, we find our way,
Through Christmas fields of purest day.
The crunch of snow beneath our feet,
The chilly air, the warmth we meet.
It all combines to show us how,
The world feels Christmas in the now.
So take a walk, enjoy the scene,
Let snowy paths feel calm, serene.
For in this journey, slow and true,
The magic of Christmas finds you.
Let every tree, let every star,
Remind us how loved we are.
For winter's walk, through frost and cold,
Brings warmth to hearts, both young and old.

# Poem 53: Christmas Magic

There's magic in the air tonight,
A wonder born of joy and light.
It dances through each home and street,
In every smile and heart we meet.
The stars above, they softly gleam,
Enhancing every Christmas dream.
While in the air, a quiet song,
Reminds us all where we belong.
It's not just gifts or shining trees,
But love that whispers on the breeze.
A kind of magic, pure and sweet,
That makes this season feel complete.
It's found in laughter, warm and true,
In every hug, between us two.
It's felt in every gentle word,
A magic touch, a love preferred.
So let this magic gently stay,
And guide us through each Christmas Day.
For in its glow, the world can see,
A love that lasts eternally.
Let Christmas magic light our way,
Through every night and shining day.
For hearts that hold its charm inside,
Will know a love that's far and wide.

# Poem 54: The Bells of Christmas Eve

The bells of Christmas Eve ring clear,
A sound that warms both far and near.
Their chimes resound through frosty air,
A melody beyond compare.
They call the weary, guide the lost,
Through snow and cold, no matter the cost.
Each toll a promise, sweet and true,
That love and peace will see us through.
The village hums with quiet cheer,
As midnight's hour draws ever near.
The bells proclaim, with voices bright,
The coming joy of Christmas light.
Through winding streets, their echoes spread,
A gentle song from overhead.
And in their sound, our hearts align,
With hope and love, a gift divine.
So let us hear their joyous song,
And let it lift our spirits strong.
For Christmas Eve, with bells that chime,
Brings peace and joy through endless time.
Their music lingers, pure and deep,
A tune of love we long to keep.
The bells of Christmas sing of grace,
And fill the world with warm embrace.

# Poem 55: Under the Mistletoe

Beneath the mistletoe we stand,
A tender kiss, a love so grand.
Its leaves a symbol, bold and green,
Of bonds unbroken, pure, serene.
A moment shared in festive glow,
Where hearts connect and feelings show.
The world beyond fades soft and slow,
As love ignites beneath its bow.
The winter chill cannot compete,
With warmth that makes our joy complete.
For every kiss beneath its charm,
Becomes a sweet and lasting balm.
It tells of love, of friendship true,
Of ties that strengthen and renew.
And as we linger, hearts in tow,
We find a peace the season shows.
So let the mistletoe remind,
Of love that's patient, pure, and kind.
For in its shadow, hearts will grow,
And cherish life's sweet mistletoe.
This simple sprig, with leaves so bright,
Holds Christmas magic every night.
Beneath its charm, let love take flight,
And shine like stars in winter's light.

# Poem 56: Christmas Candies

The candies glisten, sweet and bright,
They fill our hearts with pure delight.
From peppermint to chocolate sweet,
Each treat a joy, a festive feat.
The candy canes with stripes of red,
Are hung with care, as stories spread.
Their curves and colors, bold and true,
Bring Christmas cheer to me and you.
The truffles rich, the fudge so fine,
Each piece a taste of Christmastime.
They melt like snow upon the tongue,
A gift for old, a treat for young.
The sugared fruits, the brittle crack,
Bring memories of seasons back.
Of laughter shared and moments dear,
Each candy speaks of Christmas cheer.
So savor every bite and taste,
Let none of these sweet gifts go to waste.
For in their sweetness, we will find,
A joy that lingers in the mind.
Let Christmas candies, bright and small,
Bring love and laughter to us all.
For every sweet, in wrapper tied,
Holds holiday magic deep inside.

# Poem 57: The Stockings on the Mantel

The stockings hang in perfect line,
A Christmas tradition, pure and fine.
With names stitched tight and colors bright,
They wait for gifts on this clear night.
Each stocking holds a special place,
A token of love's warm embrace.
For young and old, they stand in cheer,
A sign that Christmas time is here.
The fireplace glows, its warmth unfolds,
As stories of the past are told.
And as we gaze at stockings near,
We feel the joy of those held dear.
In every stitch, in every seam,
A piece of Christmas joy does gleam.
For stockings filled with treats and toys,
Bring happiness to girls and boys.
But more than gifts, these socks contain,
A love that time cannot restrain.
They hang with hope, with dreams untold,
A symbol of the heart's bright gold.
So may your stockings, big or small,
Bring Christmas magic to us all.
And as they hang on this clear night,
May they be filled with love's true light.

# Poem 58: Reindeer on the Roof

Above the house, upon the sleigh,
The reindeer wait, not far away.
Their antlers glisten, frost aglow,
As winds of winter gently blow.
They stomp their hooves, they shake their heads,
They rest on rooftops, snowy beds.
Their eyes, they twinkle bright and clear,
As Christmas joy draws ever near.
With Santa's call, they leap and soar,
To travel far from shore to shore.
Through starry skies, they make their flight,
A wondrous scene on Christmas night.
Each reindeer strong, each reindeer swift,
They carry high each precious gift.
With every bound, they light the skies,
A marvel seen through children's eyes.
So if you hear a soft hoof's tap,
Or gentle thud upon your gap,
Know reindeer came with sleigh in tow,
To spread the love that we all know.
Their journey long, their purpose true,
To bring Christmas magic straight to you.
So let us honor their great flight,
These reindeer brave on Christmas night.

# Poem 59: Wrapped in Christmas Joy

The ribbons curl, the paper shines,
Each gift a treasure, love defines.
With careful hands, each present wrapped,
A token of the heart, perhaps.
The bows are tied with festive flair,
A little sparkle here and there.
For every gift beneath the tree,
Is wrapped in joy for all to see.
But more than paper, tape, and bows,
It's what inside each gift that shows.
The thought, the care, the love so true,
That makes each present feel brand new.
Unwrapping gifts, the laughter flows,
A joy that every family knows.
For giving love in boxes small,
Brings happiness to one and all.
So let each package, large or slight,
Be filled with Christmas pure and bright.
For wrapped in joy, each gift will bring,
A love that makes the spirit sing.
And when the paper's torn away,
The love remains beyond the day.
For gifts of joy, in every part,
Are treasures kept within the heart.

# Poem 60: The Night Before

The night before, the house is still,
Yet magic stirs with quiet thrill.
The stockings hang, the tree is bright,
Awaiting Santa's yearly flight.
The children sleep with dreams aglow,
Of snowy fields and gifts below.
Their whispered hopes to stars they send,
For Christmas joy that knows no end.
The fire fades, its embers gleam,
A warming glow, a soothing dream.
And in the silence, all can feel,
The spirit of the season, real.
The world prepares for morning's light,
For songs of joy and hearts so bright.
For in this calm, the love appears,
A cherished gift through all the years.
So let us pause, with hearts sincere,
To feel the peace that draws us near.
For Christmas Eve, so calm, so clear,
Brings hope and love we hold most dear.

# Poem 61: The Polar Express

A train appears through snowy haze,
Its whistle calls, its engine plays.
It journeys far through winter's land,
With dreams and magic close at hand.
The Polar Express, with shining steel,
Carries those whose hearts can feel.
A midnight ride through frosty air,
To reach a place beyond compare.
Its windows glow, its passengers cheer,
As Christmas magic draws them near.
Each stop it makes, a world unfolds,
With tales of wonder, joy untold.
Through mountains high and valleys deep,
The train speeds on, it will not sleep.
It races toward a starry gleam,
To bring us closer to the dream.
So if you hear its distant chime,
Board quick, don't wait, there's little time.
For Christmas rides the Polar Express,
A journey where pure hearts are blessed.

# Poem 62: The Village Christmas Tree

The village tree stands tall and grand,
A beacon bright in winter's land.
Its branches decked in festive cheer,
It gathers all from far and near.
The lanterns glow, the garlands shine,
Each ornament a tale divine.
And at its base, the children sing,
A chorus full of joy they bring.
The townsfolk gather, hand in hand,
To form a circle where they stand.
With every song, with every cheer,
They welcome in the Christmas year.
The star above, it crowns the tree,
A symbol of unity.
For in its light, we come to see,
The love that binds our family.
So may the tree forever shine,
A treasured gift, a hope divine.
For every village, big or small,
Finds joy in Christmas' loving call.

# Poem 63: A Christmas Letter

Dear friends and family, near and far,
You light our lives like Christmas stars.
This season brings a chance to say,
We hold you close in every way.
The year has passed with trials, cheers,
Through ups and downs, through hopes and fears.
But now we pause to send our love,
And blessings from the stars above.
May every home be filled with light,
With laughter ringing through the night.
And may your hearts, so pure, so true,
Find peace and joy the whole year through.
For Christmas time, with all its grace,
Is found within the smiles we place.
And as we write these words sincere,
We wish you love this coming year.
So read this letter, sent with care,
And know we're with you everywhere.
For Christmas ties both near and far,
In bonds as bright as any star.

# Poem 64: The Snow Globe's Tale

Inside the globe, a world appears,
A timeless land of love and cheers.
With every shake, the snowflakes fall,
A wintry wonderland for all.
A tiny house, a glowing light,
A family gathers in the night.
Their laughter rings, their spirits soar,
As snow drifts soft around their door.
The village square, the trees adorned,
The carolers sing, the hearts are warmed.
Each figure frozen in its place,
Yet filled with life, with joy, with grace.
The globe, a keepsake on the shelf,
Holds Christmas in a world itself.
And as we gaze, it stirs our soul,
A vision of a season whole.
So let the snow globe gently spin,
And watch the magic dance within.
For every flake, each tiny tale,
Brings Christmas joy that will not fail.
The snow globe's charm, a treasured art,
Holds Christmas close within the heart.
A little world, yet vast and wide,
Where dreams of love and peace reside.

# Poem 65: The Christmas Star

The Christmas star, it shines so bright,
A guiding flame through winter's night.
It led the wise on journey's way,
To find a child on Christmas Day.
Its light now glows in every sky,
A beacon seen by you and I.
It calls us forth, with hearts sincere,
To find the love that draws us near.
Through years and miles, it leads us still,
Through every joy, through every hill.
It whispers softly in the dark,
A light of hope, a simple spark.
The Christmas star, a tale retold,
Of faith and love that's pure as gold.
It shines above, both calm and clear,
To guide us through another year.
So as you gaze at stars tonight,
Let Christmas fill your heart with light.
For in their glow, we come to see,
The path of peace and harmony.
May every star, both near and far,
Remind you of the Christmas star.
Its message pure, its promise true,
A gift of love for me and you.

# Poem 66: The Christmas Feast

The table set, the candles glow,
A festive warmth begins to grow.
With every dish, with every plate,
We gather 'round to celebrate.
The turkey roasts, the pudding steams,
A feast beyond our wildest dreams.
From savory bites to sweets so fine,
Each taste is touched with love divine.
We pass the bread, we raise a toast,
To family here we cherish most.
Each laugh, each story that we share,
Shows Christmas love beyond compare.
The feast is more than food and wine,
It's moments spent where hearts align.
For every meal, a memory made,
A cherished scene that won't soon fade.
So let us savor every bite,
And bask in joy this Christmas night.
For at this feast, with loved ones near,
We find the gift of Christmas cheer.
The table full, the spirits high,
The love we share will never die.
For Christmas feasts, both rich and sweet,
Are where our souls and hearts do meet.

# Poem 67: Santa's Workshop

At the North Pole, beneath the snow,
There's magic in the workshop's glow.
The elves all bustle, day and night,
To bring the world its Christmas light.
They craft the toys with skillful hands,
For children's dreams in far-off lands.
Each doll, each train, each teddy bear,
Is made with love and tender care.
The hammers ring, the laughter flies,
As reindeer watch with knowing eyes.
They'll take these treasures on their way,
To spread the joy on Christmas Day.
Santa checks his list with pride,
His sleigh prepared for a global ride.
And as he laughs, the elves all cheer,
For Christmas Eve is finally here.
The workshop hums with festive cheer,
A place where joy is engineered.
For every gift that's made tonight,
Carries the world's purest delight.
So as you dream on Christmas Eve,
Know Santa's elves will not deceive.
For in their hands, your wishes stay,
To bring you joy on Christmas Day.

# Poem 68: The Christmas Wreath

Upon the door, the wreath is hung,
Its evergreen with ribbons strung.
A symbol bold, a circle true,
Of life and love for me and you.
Its boughs of pine, so rich, so green,
A festive touch, serene and keen.
It welcomes all who come to stay,
And shares the joy of Christmas Day.
The holly's red, the berries bright,
Bring nature's charm to winter's night.
While every bow, so neatly tied,
Reflects the warmth we hold inside.
It tells a tale of endless cheer,
A sign of hope through every year.
For as the seasons come and go,
The wreath remains, through frost and snow.
So may its circle gently show,
The love that makes our spirits glow.
For in its form, we come to see,
The boundless joy of unity.
Let every wreath, on every door,
Spread Christmas love forevermore.
A simple sign, yet oh so grand,
Of peace and joy in every land.

# Poem 69: The Quiet of Christmas Night

The world is hushed on Christmas night,
A peaceful calm, a pure delight.
The snow lies still, the stars shine clear,
As silent whispers draw us near.
The hustle fades, the lights grow dim,
A moment soft, a sacred hymn.
And in this quiet, hearts can hear,
The true message of Christmas cheer.
It's found in stillness, calm and sweet,
In every breath, a quiet beat.
A gentle love, a whispered grace,
That fills each home, each heart, each space.
The quiet speaks of peace profound,
A harmony in every sound.
It wraps us close, it holds us tight,
A gift of rest on Christmas night.
So let this peace within us stay,
And guide us through each coming day.
For in this quiet, soft and true,
The heart of Christmas shines anew.
Let every soul find peace tonight,
In Christmas calm, in soft moonlight.
For quiet brings a love so deep,
That Christmas joy in hearts will keep.

# Poem 70: Frost on the Windowpane

The frost upon the window glows,
A canvas where the winter shows.
With every swirl, with every line,
It paints a scene of Christmas time.
The icy patterns softly gleam,
Like fragile lace, a snowy dream.
Each crystal form, a fleeting art,
A winter's touch, a frozen heart.
Through frosted glass, we see the night,
A world transformed in silver light.
The stars above, the snow below,
Combine to make the season glow.
The warmth inside, the cold without,
Creates a bond, dispels the doubt.
For even frost, with chilling hand,
Brings beauty to this festive land.
So as we gaze at winter's art,
Let frost inspire a warming heart.
For in its chill, a truth remains,
That love endures through frosted panes.
Let every flake, let every line,
Remind us of a love divine.
For Christmas lives in icy frames,
Through winter's art and frost's soft claims.

# Poem 71: The Gift of Light

The gift of light, so pure, so warm,
Transforms the night, dispels the storm.
In every home, its glow is seen,
A beacon bright, a love serene.
The candles flicker, lanterns gleam,
A gentle glow, a soothing dream.
They light the tree, they frame the door,
And spread their warmth across the floor.
Each spark, a promise softly made,
To guide us through both light and shade.
For Christmas light, though small it seems,
Can kindle hearts and fuel our dreams.
It shines in laughter, shines in care,
It lives in every love we share.
A flame that never fades away,
But grows with every passing day.
So may this light forever glow,
And through our lives its beauty show.
For in its warmth, our souls unite,
To share the gift of Christmas light.
Let every lamp, let every spark,
Illuminate the deepest dark.
For Christmas light, both calm and bright,
Will guide us through the longest night.

# Poem 72: The Chimney's Tale

The chimney stands, both tall and wide,
A secret path where dreams reside.
It waits in silence through the night,
To guide Saint Nick on his grand flight.
The hearth below, its embers glow,
A cozy warmth as soft winds blow.
The stockings hang in perfect line,
Awaiting gifts, a joyful sign.
Above, the stars light up the skies,
But in the hearth, a magic lies.
For every year, through frost and snow,
The chimney tells of love's pure glow.
Its bricks have seen both young and old,
Through Christmas stories often told.
Each year it keeps the flame alive,
A symbol of the joy we strive.
So as we gather near its flame,
Let's cherish all that it proclaims.
For chimneys hold a tale so sweet,
Of Christmas love that can't be beat.
Let every hearth, both great and small,
Bring warmth and peace to one and all.
For in their glow, we come to see,
The magic of our family tree.

# Poem 73: Midnight Snowfall

At midnight strikes, the snowfall comes,
Its gentle hush, like distant drums.
The world is wrapped in silent white,
A wonderland on Christmas night.
Each flake descends in graceful flight,
A dance of peace in purest light.
It settles soft on bough and stone,
Transforming all the earth has known.
The streets now gleam, the rooftops shine,
A scene of beauty, so divine.
And as the snow falls, calm and slow,
It carries whispers we all know.
A wish for love, a hope for peace,
A moment when all fears release.
For in this quiet, hearts can hear,
The song of Christmas drawing near.
So let us stand and watch the skies,
As midnight snow before us flies.
For every flake, so soft, so bright,
Brings Christmas dreams to life tonight.
Let snowfall weave its tender tale,
Of love that never will grow stale.
And through the night, let spirits soar,
To find the peace we're searching for.

# Poem 74: The Joy of Togetherness

At Christmas time, we come to find,
The joy of love that ties and binds.
Through every laugh, through every cheer,
Togetherness draws us near.
Around the tree, we gather close,
With those we love, with those we chose.
Each moment shared, each hand we hold,
Becomes a memory, pure as gold.
It's in the meals, the games we play,
The simple joys that light our way.
No need for grandeur, wealth, or fame,
Togetherness is life's true flame.
We share our hopes, we share our dreams,
We share the magic Christmas brings.
For when we're near, both young and old,
We find a warmth that can't grow cold.
So let this season's lesson stay,
To cherish those who bless our day.
For Christmas joy is fully known,
When hearts are joined, and love has grown.
In every hug, in every smile,
Togetherness makes life worthwhile.
And in this love, we come to see,
The beauty of our unity.

# Poem 75: Sleigh Ride Through the Snow

The sleigh bells ring, the horses neigh,
As we embark on wintry play.
Through snowy fields, through forests wide,
We take a joyful sleigh ride.
The cold winds nip, the snowflakes fall,
Yet laughter warms the hearts of all.
With blankets wrapped and spirits high,
We race beneath the starlit sky.
The reins are pulled, the sleigh glides fast,
Through frozen streams and meadows vast.
Each bump, each turn, brings squeals of glee,
As trees blur past in snowy sea.
The jingle bells keep time in tune,
Their music echoes with the moon.
A festive song, a joyful beat,
That makes our Christmas ride complete.
So hold on tight, let laughter flow,
And feel the thrill of sleigh bells' show.
For in this ride, we come to see,
The joy of winter's revelry.
Let every sleigh, let every cheer,
Bring Christmas magic ever near.
For sleigh rides through the snow so bright,
Fill every heart with pure delight.

# Poem 76: The Christmas Quilt

The quilt is spread, its colors bright,
A tapestry of love's delight.
Each patch a tale, a memory dear,
That weaves the threads of Christmas cheer.
It wraps us close on frosty nights,
With stories stitched in patterned lights.
A piece of red, a square of green,
Recall the joys that once have been.
The laughter shared, the tears we've dried,
The moments spent with hearts open wide.
This quilt enfolds both young and old,
In warmth that never will grow cold.
Its threads are strong, its fabric true,
A symbol of the love we knew.
And every year, when Christmas calls,
The quilt brings peace within its walls.
So as we rest beneath its care,
We feel the love that's always there.
For Christmas quilts, though soft and small,
Hold memories that bless us all.
Let every stitch, let every seam,
Protect the heart, fulfill the dream.
For in this quilt, we come to find,
The ties that bind through all of time.

# Poem 77: The Christmas Parade

The Christmas parade rolls down the street,
With marching bands and drums that beat.
The floats are decked in lights so grand,
A festive sight, a wonderland.
The children wave, their faces glow,
As candy canes and toys bestow.
Each float a scene of Christmas lore,
From reindeer sleighs to elves' toy stores.
The music plays, the trumpets blare,
A joyful tune fills frosty air.
And as the parade winds its way through,
It spreads the spirit, bold and true.
The crowd joins in with cheers and song,
As Santa's float comes rolling strong.
With jolly laugh and "Ho, ho, ho!"
He waves to all who stand below.
The Christmas parade, both bright and loud,
Brings smiles to every gathered crowd.
It's more than floats, it's more than cheer,
It's love and joy that draws us near.
So let us treasure this grand display,
A festive gift on Christmas Day.
For in its march, we come to see,
The beauty of community.

# Poem 78: The Sound of Christmas Morning

The morning breaks, the day is here,
A time of joy, of love, and cheer.
The house is filled with laughter sweet,
As little feet begin to meet.
The rustle of the paper bright,
As gifts are opened with delight.
The clatter soft of toys in hand,
A symphony so simply grand.
The smell of breakfast fills the air,
Of pancakes stacked and cocoa's flare.
Each sound and scent, a festive song,
That draws our hearts where they belong.
The chorus rises, soft and clear,
Of voices loved, both far and near.
For Christmas morning's gentle tune,
Is like the glow of winter's moon.
So let us savor every sound,
For Christmas magic does abound.
In every laugh, in every cheer,
The spirit sings for all to hear.
May every morning bring this light,
And fill our days with pure delight.
For Christmas sounds, both near and far,
Are melodies of who we are.

# Poem 79: The Tree in the Square

In the town square, the tree stands tall,
A gathering place for one and all.
Its boughs adorned with shining lights,
A beacon on these winter nights.
Around its base, the people meet,
With smiles so warm and hearts that greet.
Their voices rise in joyful song,
As Christmas brings them all along.
The star atop, it gleams with pride,
A symbol strong, a love worldwide.
And as the tree glows ever bright,
It fills the square with pure delight.
The children play, the elders cheer,
For Christmas time is finally here.
This tree, a gift to all who see,
Brings hope and joy to you and me.
So let it shine through winter's chill,
A tree of peace, a symbol still.
For in its light, the world can share,
The magic found in the town square.
May every square, in every land,
Hold Christmas close, a love so grand.
For trees that stand with lights so fair,
Bring unity beyond compare.

# Poem 80: Candy Cane Dreams

The candy canes hang neat and sweet,
A Christmas treat that can't be beat.
With stripes of red and white so bright,
They sparkle in the twinkling light.
Each curve a swirl of peppermint,
A flavor fresh, a festive hint.
They dangle from the Christmas tree,
A symbol of sweet unity.
In stockings hung by fire's warm glow,
Or wrapped as gifts for friends to know.
Their simple charm, their sweetness clear,
Brings Christmas joy to all who're near.
With every bite, a dream unfolds,
Of snowy lands and tales retold.
For candy canes, both small and grand,
Hold magic crafted hand in hand.
So may your Christmas be as sweet,
As every cane, a special treat.
For in their stripes, we see the love,
That graces us from skies above.
Let candy canes bring joy supreme,
And fill your nights with peppermint dreams.
For Christmas tastes, both rich and rare,
Are gifts of love beyond compare.

# Poem 81: Under Winter's Sky

Beneath the vast and starry dome,
The world feels close, the world feels home.
The winter sky, both calm and wide,
Reflects the love we hold inside.
The constellations softly shine,
A universe in grand design.
And as we gaze with wonder high,
Our hearts align beneath the sky.
The snow below, the stars above,
Create a scene of peace and love.
Each flake, each light, a gentle part,
Of Christmas woven through the heart.
We stand together, hand in hand,
And feel the warmth of winter's land.
For under skies of velvet blue,
The world seems fresh, the world seems new.
So may this sky remind us all,
Of blessings big and moments small.
For in its depth, we come to see,
The endless bonds of you and me.
Let every star, let every breeze,
Bring joy that lingers, love that frees.
For under winter's starry sky,
The spirit of Christmas will never die.

# Poem 82: The Gingerbread House

The gingerbread house stands sweet and strong,
A festive treat we've built so long.
With candy roofs and sugar walls,
It lights the room as snowflakes fall.
Each gumdrop placed, each frosting swirl,
Adds charm to this delicious world.
The windows bright with icing trim,
Reflect the joy that lives within.
We gather 'round with careful hand,
To craft a house that's simply grand.
Its scent of spice, its look of cheer,
Brings Christmas magic ever near.
Though houses crumble, treats are eaten,
The memories stay, they won't be beaten.
For in this act, both young and old,
Find joy that's sweet, a love untold.
So let us bake and build with glee,
A gingerbread for all to see.
For in its walls, we come to find,
A Christmas warmth that's one of a kind.
May every house, both big and small,
Bring happiness to one and all.
For gingerbread, in festive light,
Brings Christmas dreams both pure and bright.

# Poem 83: Christmas Wishes

On Christmas Eve, we close our eyes,
And send our wishes to the skies.
We hope for love, we hope for cheer,
We wish for joy throughout the year.
A wish for peace in every land,
For hearts united, hand in hand.
A wish for those who feel alone,
To find a love they've never known.
We wish for health, for laughter sweet,
For kindness shown in every street.
A world where hope will never fade,
Where dreams are real and love is made.
These Christmas wishes, bold and true,
Are whispers sent from me to you.
And as the stars shine clear above,
They carry all our hopes with love.
So let your wishes take their flight,
On this calm, sacred Christmas night.
For every wish, so soft, so dear,
Brings light and joy throughout the year.
May every heart, both near and far,
Feel Christmas wishes like a star.
For in these dreams, the world can see,
A future bright for you and me.

# Poem 84: The Nativity Scene

The stable stands, both humble and small,
Yet holds the greatest gift of all.
A manger low, a baby cries,
Beneath the stars in peaceful skies.
The shepherds come, their hearts so pure,
To witness love that will endure.
They kneel in awe, their spirits bright,
As angels sing on this clear night.
The wise men travel, guided far,
By heaven's light, the Christmas star.
With gifts of gold, frankincense, myrrh,
They honor Him, the world's great stir.
The animals rest, the air is still,
The world awakens to God's will.
For in this scene, both near and far,
Shines love that time cannot mar.
So may we keep this story close,
A tale of peace the world needs most.
For in the manger's quiet grace,
We find the light of love's embrace.
Let every nativity remind,
The humble birth of love divine.
For Christmas starts in hearts so true,
With peace that's born anew in you.

# Poem 85: The Christmas Carol

A simple tune begins to play,
It whispers soft, then sweeps away.
The carol sings of joy and peace,
Of love that grows and won't decease.
Its melody, so sweet, so clear,
Fills every home with Christmas cheer.
Through frosty air, through candlelight,
It warms the soul on winter's night.
The lyrics tell of stars above,
Of angels' songs and endless love.
Each note a thread in joy's embrace,
A harmony of Christmas grace.
The carol travels far and near,
Uniting hearts with festive cheer.
For in its song, a truth we find,
That love can heal and free the mind.
So let the carols softly ring,
And let your heart with gladness sing.
For Christmas music, pure and bright,
Brings hope and love on this clear night.
May every song, both loud and small,
Spread Christmas peace to one and all.
For in their tunes, the world can see,
A season bright with harmony.

# Poem 86: The Christmas Lantern

The lantern shines through frosty haze,
Its golden light a warming blaze.
It stands beside the old front door,
A beacon bright for evermore.
Its glass reflects the snowy ground,
While soft within, its glow is found.
It calls to travelers passing by,
To find their rest where love is nigh.
The lantern speaks in quiet flame,
A timeless tale, a gentle claim.
Of nights long past, of hearts drawn near,
To share in Christmas warmth sincere.
Its light will never fade or die,
Through storm and chill, it lights the sky.
A symbol of the hope we keep,
A promise strong through slumber deep.
So let your lantern brightly burn,
And guide the weary who return.
For in its glow, the world will see,
The heart of Christmas charity.
May every home, with lantern bright,
Shine forth with love on Christmas night.
And in its flame, may joy reside,
A warmth that never will subside.

# Poem 87: The Angel's Watch

The angel stands atop the tree,
A symbol of eternity.
With golden wings and eyes so kind,
She watches over all mankind.
Her presence brings a peaceful glow,
A comfort deep, a love we know.
For angels guard both night and day,
And guide us on life's winding way.
She carries messages of cheer,
Of hope and joy this time of year.
Her silent gaze, her gentle grace,
Reflects the light of love's embrace.
Through every trial, every fear,
The angel's watch keeps spirits near.
For in her care, our hearts are free,
To share in Christmas harmony.
So let her light shine ever clear,
A beacon bright, a guide sincere.
For angels walk among us still,
With hearts of peace and hands of will.
And as she stands, so calm, so true,
The Christmas angel watches you.
A guardian kind, a friend so near,
Brings love and hope this time of year.

# Poem 88: The Ice Skaters

The frozen pond, a crystal stage,
Reflects the glow of winter's page.
The skaters glide, their laughter rings,
A melody of joyful things.
With every turn, with every spin,
Their hearts take flight, their smiles begin.
The ice beneath, so smooth, so clear,
Carries the sound of festive cheer.
They twirl as one, they move as free,
A dance of grace for all to see.
Their scarves trail long, their mittens fly,
Beneath the starlit Christmas sky.
The cold may bite, the wind may blow,
Yet warmth within will always grow.
For in this dance, in winter's play,
They find the joy of Christmas Day.
So let the skaters softly glide,
Through snowy fields, through Christmastide.
For in their steps, we come to know,
The beauty found in ice and snow.
May every pond, both small and grand,
Bring joy that only hearts understand.
For Christmas lives in every cheer,
And skates upon the ice so clear.

# Poem 89: The Joyful Reunion

The train arrives, the doors swing wide,
A rush of warmth from those inside.
With open arms and faces bright,
We greet our loved ones on this night.
The hugs are tight, the laughter flows,
A love that only distance grows.
For every mile, for every year,
The bond remains as strong and clear.
The house is filled with voices sweet,
As hearts and hands in joy do meet.
The stories shared, the memories made,
Bring light that will not fade or fade.
The reunion's gift, a priceless one,
A love that's never come undone.
For Christmas brings us all together,
Through every storm, through every weather.
So cherish those who gather near,
And hold them close, both far and dear.
For joyful reunions light the way,
To celebrate this Christmas Day.
May every heart, in every place,
Find comfort in a warm embrace.
For Christmas joy is best when shared,
With those whose love has always cared.

# Poem 90: The Christmas Candle

The candle flickers, soft and low,
Its gentle flame, a steady glow.
It casts a light both pure and bright,
A beacon on this Christmas night.
Its wax melts slow, its warmth extends,
A quiet peace it gently sends.
It lights the way for hearts to see,
The love that burns eternally.
In every room, it softly beams,
A witness to our hopes and dreams.
Its glow reflects on faces near,
A light that draws all close and dear.
The candle tells of silent grace,
Of joy that time cannot erase.
It warms the heart, it soothes the soul,
A guiding light to make us whole.
So let your candle brightly shine,
A symbol of the love divine.
For in its flame, we find the spark,
That lights the way through winter's dark.
May every candle, great and small,
Bring peace and hope to one and all.
For Christmas candles softly say,
That love will guide us every day.

# Poem 91: St. Nicholas' Visit

The clock strikes twelve, the house is still,
But magic stirs on windowsill.
With sleigh and reindeer, swift and light,
St. Nicholas arrives tonight.
He slides down chimneys, one by one,
His work of joy has just begun.
With sack in hand, he moves with care,
And leaves his gifts for all to share.
The stockings full, the tree aglow,
He smiles, his cheeks a rosy show.
His laughter soft, his spirit high,
He spreads his love beneath the sky.
He takes a moment, nods his head,
Then through the chimney he is led.
With reindeer ready, sleigh in tow,
He whispers softly, "Ho, ho, ho!"
And as he soars through frosty air,
He leaves behind his Christmas care.
For every home, both far and near,
Will feel his love this time of year.
So as you sleep, know he'll arrive,
To make the season come alive.
For St. Nicholas, with heart so true,
Brings Christmas magic straight to you.

# Poem 92: The Christmas Clock

The Christmas clock ticks soft and slow,
Its golden hands, a steady flow.
It counts the moments, one by one,
Until the Christmas morn is spun.
Its chime rings clear on midnight's toll,
A signal for each waiting soul.
For when it strikes, the world will see,
The joy of Christmas, wild and free.
Through every hour, it gently speaks,
Of peace and love the season seeks.
Its rhythm, like a heartbeat strong,
Keeps time with carols, sweet and long.
The clock reminds us, year by year,
That Christmas magic draws us near.
No matter where, no matter when,
Its chime brings love to hearts again.
So listen close, let moments stay,
As Christmas time leads on the way.
For in its hands, the world will find,
The gift of time, a love unlined.
Let every tick, let every chime,
Proclaim the joy of Christmastime.
For Christmas clocks, both old and new,
Bring timeless blessings straight to you.

# Poem 93: The Snow Angel

Upon the snow, so soft and white,
A figure forms in morning light.
With arms outstretched and wings so wide,
A snow angel stands by our side.
The children laugh, their voices sing,
As snowflakes dance and soft winds cling.
They shape the snow with joy and care,
Creating beauty everywhere.
The angel's form, both calm and true,
Reflects the love of skies so blue.
A guardian made of winter's grace,
A symbol of this sacred space.
It whispers peace, it brings us cheer,
A friend that's only seen this year.
And though it melts as seasons turn,
Its memory will always burn.
So let us craft with hands of light,
A snow angel on this cold night.
For in its shape, our hearts will see,
The simple joy of purity.
May every angel, bold or small,
Bring peace and warmth to one and all.
For snow angels remind us why,
Christmas love will never die.

# Poem 94: The Toymaker's Gift

The toymaker hums as he works late,
With hands that craft each child's fate.
His shop aglow with tools and care,
Creates the toys that bring us there.
A wooden horse, a soldier bright,
A doll with eyes that gleam with light.
Each piece he builds with steady hand,
A marvel born from heart and plan.
The shelves are filled, the work complete,
A world of joy for all to meet.
For in his craft, the love does show,
A gift of care for those who know.
The toymaker smiles, his task now done,
As stars rise high and greet the sun.
For every toy, both near and far,
Carries a light like Christmas star.
So cherish gifts made with the heart,
For they're a treasure from the start.
The toymaker's gift, both true and bright,
Brings Christmas wonder to the night.
May every toy, in every hand,
Bring joy and love across the land.
For in their play, the world can see,
The spirit of the Christmas tree.

# Poem 95: The Holly Crown

A crown of holly, bold and green,
Adorns the table, pure and clean.
Its berries red, its leaves so fine,
A symbol of the Christmastime.
It circles round in perfect grace,
A sign of love in every place.
For holly, with its sharp-edged leaves,
Reminds us of the joy that weaves.
The crown speaks softly, calm and clear,
Of peace that grows this time of year.
It crowns the hearts of all who share,
A love that reaches everywhere.
So let it rest on heads or doors,
A wreath that opens endless shores.
For in its form, we come to see,
The lasting light of unity.
May every holly crown remind,
Of blessings rich and ties that bind.
For Christmas crowns, both green and bright,
Bring warmth and peace on this clear night.
And as it shines in candle's glow,
It spreads the love that we all know.
For holly crowns, with grace so true,
Are Christmas blessings meant for you.

# Poem 96: The Christmas Sleigh

The sleigh stands ready, painted bright,
Its runners gleam in moon's soft light.
A sturdy frame, a cushioned seat,
Awaits the journey, pure and sweet.
The horses neigh, their breaths like mist,
The reins are tied, the bells are kissed.
With jingling notes and steady pace,
The sleigh begins its joyful race.
Through snowy fields and frosty trees,
It glides with ease on winter's breeze.
The stars above, they softly guide,
The sleigh through Christmas countryside.
The laughter rings, the voices sing,
As love and cheer the journey bring.
For in this ride, both fast and slow,
The Christmas spirit starts to glow.
So let the sleigh through snowflakes dart,
And carry joy to every heart.
For Christmas rides, both far and near,
Bring warmth and love to all who hear.
May every sleigh, with bells in tune,
Bring Christmas magic 'neath the moon.
A ride that lifts the soul so high,
And brings the stars within the sky.

# Poem 97: The Fireplace Glow

The fireplace crackles, embers glow,
A warming light through frosty snow.
Its flames reach high, its sparks take flight,
A beacon on this Christmas night.
Around its warmth, we gather near,
To share our stories, spread our cheer.
The logs burn bright, their whispers hum,
Of winter nights both yet to come.
The stockings hang in cozy line,
Awaiting gifts of Christmas time.
While every flicker, every spark,
Brings comfort to the cold and dark.
Its heat reminds us of the love,
That warms our hearts, sent from above.
For in its light, we come to see,
The strength of family unity.
So may your fireplace softly burn,
As Christmas joy takes its return.
For in its glow, both young and old,
Find warmth that never will grow cold.
Let every hearth, both big and small,
Bring peace and joy to one and all.
For fireplace glow, with steady flame,
Keeps Christmas love forever the same.

# Poem 98: The Christmas Postman

The postman trudges through the snow,
With bags of letters, gifts in tow.
His steps are sure, his mission clear,
To spread the joy of Christmas cheer.
From house to house, he makes his way,
Delivering love on Christmas Day.
Each card, each note, a message true,
From friends afar, from me to you.
His coat is dusted white with frost,
Yet through the chill, he's never lost.
For every letter in his hand,
Connects the hearts across the land.
He hums a carol, soft and light,
As stars above shine through the night.
For in his work, he plays a part,
In sharing joy from heart to heart.
So thank the postman when he's near,
For carrying hope this time of year.
For every step through winter's chill,
He brings a love that lingers still.
May every letter, every line,
Bring warmth like mulled and spiced wine.
For Christmas post, both far and wide,
Spreads joy and peace through Christmastide.

# Poem 99: The Carol Singers

They walk through streets on frosty nights,
Their voices clear, their spirits bright.
The carol singers, bold and true,
Bring Christmas joy to me and you.
With lanterns held and scarves wrapped tight,
They sing beneath the soft starlight.
Each note, each word, a gift they share,
A melody beyond compare.
The songs of old, the hymns of peace,
Through quiet streets, their echoes crease.
Their harmonies lift hearts so high,
And brighten every passerby.
A knock on doors, a tune well played,
Their cheerful songs, a sweet cascade.
For in their music, love does flow,
A warmth that melts the coldest snow.
So let us sing with voices strong,
And join the carol singers' throng.
For Christmas carols, pure and sweet,
Bring unity in every street.
May every house, may every hall,
Resound with love for one and all.
For carol singers, brave and true,
Bring Christmas light to all they do.

# Poem 100: Under the Mistletoe

Under the mistletoe we meet,
Our hearts aligned, our love complete.
Its leaves above, its berries red,
A symbol of the words unsaid.
In every kiss, a promise made,
Of love that never will degrade.
Through winter's chill, through summer's heat,
This vow we keep with hearts so sweet.
The world may turn, the years may fly,
But mistletoe will never die.
It holds the magic, strong and clear,
That binds our souls each passing year.
So let us linger, side by side,
And let love's warmth through us abide.
For under mistletoe's soft glow,
The greatest gift is love we show.
This sprig of green, this simple vine,
Holds Christmas magic, pure, divine.
A kiss beneath, a love so true,
Forever starts with me and you.
Let every home, let every heart,
Embrace the love that it imparts.
For mistletoe, both high and low,
Keeps Christmas love in steady flow.

www.ingramcontent.com/pod-product-compliance
Lightning Source LLC
Chambersburg PA
CBHW050545160726

48003CB00002B/765